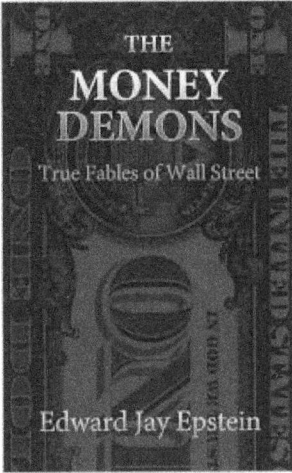

THE MONEY DEMONS: TRUE FABLES OF WALL STREET

By Edward Jay Epstein

An EJE Original

Other Books By

Inquest
Legend
News From Nowhere
The Rise and Fall of Diamonds
Agency of Fear
Between Fact and Fiction
The Assassination Chronicles
The Big Picture
The Hollywood Economist
Myths of the Media
Deception: The Invisible war Between the CIA and the KGB
Three Days In May: Sex, Surveillance and DSK

Annals of Unsolved Crime

EJE Originals

James Jesus Angleton: Was He Right?
Armand Hammer: The Darker Side
The Rockefellers
The JFK Assassination Theories
Garrison's Game
Zia's Crash
Who Killed God's Banker
The Crude Cartel
Tabloid America: Crimes of the Press
New From Nowhere Now

Copyright © by EJE Publication 2011
All Rights Reserved
ISBN 9781617040801

Parts of this book appeared in *Harpers, Manhattan, Inc,* and *The Institutional Investor*
Cover Design by Jennifer Kim

For James Q. Wilson

"Mammon is the name of a demon"
    – Nicolaus Lyranus

CONTENTS

Preface   *The Greater Fool Theory Reconsidered*

The cause of the 2008 financial crisis in America was a giant credit bubble. It was pumped up to the breaking point by a staggering $11.8 trillion in US mortgages. Americans took out these mortgages to buy, furnish, and improves homes so that they could live better than they could otherwise afford on their earnings. Indeed, they had borrowed so much money from the global banking system that by 2005 that the savings rate actually went negative for the first time since the Great Depression. This meant that Americans were borrowing and spending more than they were earning. They assumed they could pay back the loans for their dream homes because they would eternally gain in value and that they could always find a buyer willing to pay a higher price. So borrowing was rationalized by subscribing to the Greater Fool theory.

Unfortunately, in 2008, the Greater Fool theory failed. Sellers could not find buyers as home prices fell, wiping out trillions of dollars in notional value. The credit bubble had finally burst. The consequences were catastrophic. The banking system was paralyzed, if not insolvent. Millions who had been employed servicing the bubble economy now lost their jobs. The stock market crashed. The central banks had to print trillions of dollars to prevent a total global economic collapse.

But who was responsible for this disastrous credit bubble? Had unscrupulous financiers tempted people to borrow more than they could afford so they could enhance their standard of living? Had greedy manipulators rigged prices to go down so they could profit? Had evil conspirators on Wall Street caused the greater fool theory to fail? The Chinese believe in a Money Demons. So may journalists and other moralists.

The alternative explanation is that complex systems that service the quest for wealth are prone to unexpected failures.

[1]
Stalking The Giant Vampire Squid

After the near-collapse of the global financial system in September 2008, and the loss of some 8 million jobs in America, journalism searched furiously for the guilty party.   The proximate source of the crises clearly was the bankruptcy of Lehman Bros, which had been part of what remained of the-called shadow banking network. The three other financial houses in it were Morgan Stanley, Merrill Lynch, and Goldman. Unlike chartered banks, these financial entities were not directly regulated by the Federal Reserve Bank, which meant that they could profit from enormously leveraging their assets. They had assisted the chartered banks in leveraging themselves by engaging in something called "securitization."   Through this form of financial alchemy, they turned debt obligations, such as mortgages, student loans, and credit card borrowing, into securities that could be sold to other financial institutions around the globe in giant packages called Collaterized Debt Obligations, or CDOs. These creations were "structured" for rating agencies by slicing them into tiers and adding derivatives to protect against a default. These maneuvers enable them to get ratings so institutions could buy them and, since they paid a slightly higher interest rate than conventional debt, there was no shortage of buyers. And once loans were taken off the books of banks and sold as securities, banks were free to borrow more money, and lend it out, and feed the growing credit bubble until it burst.

Only one shadow bank survived the credit bubble without having to merge with another bank. It was Goldman, which was also the richest and most politically connected one, So, soon after the crash, it became a prime target of investigative journalists. "The first thing you need to know about Goldman is that it's everywhere," Matt Taibbi wrote in Rolling Stone. He then famously described it as "a great vampire squid wrapped around the face of humanity." Even though the metaphor was strained– vampire squids are tiny cephalopod that do not wrap themselves around human faces– its colorful imagery resonated throughout the media. So did many of his charges, including his contention that it had so corrupted the US government through its revolving door with the Treasury that it had received 100 cents on the dollar for CDOs that had lost most of their value. This powerful charge, enhanced with the image of a blood-sucking vampire creature, had such power in the press that even Nobel Laureate economist Paul Krugman wrote in his column the *New York Times*, "Taxpayers not only ended up honoring foolish promises made by other people, they ended up doing so at 100 cents on the dollar," adding "By making what was in effect a multibillion-dollar gift to Wall Street, policy makers undermined their own credibility — and put the broader economy at risk." The problem with this elegant indictment is that it simply is not true. The government did not make a "gift" to Goldman or the other 15 banks. Nor did it ever pay Goldman or any of the other banks, "100 cents on the dollar." Here is what happened. The NY Federal Reserve Bank, through a vehicle it set up called "Maiden Lane III," bought the $62.1 billion of CDOs from all 16 banks for $29.1 billion, or about 48 cents on a dollar. These CDOs had been fully guaranteed by the insurance giant AIG via credit default swaps. So when they declined in value AIG put up cash as margin at Goldman and other banks. These payments from AIG amounted to about 50 cents on the dollar. So it was AIG, not the government, who suffered the loss from the drop in value. The Fed, which bought them at their market value, did not lose a penny on them. None of the CDOs defaulted, and, to date, the Fed shows a $10.2 billion profit on them, while it continued to collect interest. (Indeed, they turned out be such a good investment that in 2011, AIG attempted to re-purchase them, but the Fed refused.) Goldman, despite the media focus, was actually a minor player in the deal. Two-thirds of these CDOS were held by 12 foreign-owned banks, and the single largest holder was the French bank Societe Generale SA. Since Societe Generale had informed the Fed that its regulators in France would not permit it to sell the CDOs below their market price, the Fed had little choice in the matter. It bought the CDOs at a less than 50 cents on the dollars and as a result made a multibillion dollar profit and avoided the collapse of world banking.

Another charge leveled against the Giant Vampire Squid was that it helped bring about the bursting of the subprime bubble by deliberately designing its financial vehicles to fail. This bit of demonization had its origin in a SEC civil fraud suit against Goldman in April 2010 concerning a Goldman entity called the Abacus 2007-AC1 fund. Again, Krugman is worth citing since he said the complaint effectively accused Goldman of criminal sabotage. "The SEC is charging that Goldman created and marketed securities that were deliberately designed to fail, so that an important client could make money off that failure," Krugman wrote in the *New York Times*. "That's what I would call looting."

However, the cited SEC complaint did not allege that Goldman deliberately designed the fund to fail. What it alleges is that Goldman failed to disclose material information the prospectus concerning the role played in the fund's creation by one of its four participants, John Paulson. According to the complaint, in 2007 Paulson, a large hedge fund operator, wanted to make a billion dollar wager that subprime-backed mortgages would collapse. So he went to Goldman , which, like the other major financial houses, is in the business of creating such customized gambling products for clients, and paid it a $15 million fee to created Abacus 2007-AC1. The singular purpose of this fund was to provide exposure to subprime home mortgage-backed securities. If the underlying 90 securities did not default, those who were optimistic about the housing market, and took the long side of Abacus, would collect handsome profits. If the housing bubble burst, Paulson, who took the entire short side, would make the profit. Despite its complexity, it was nothing more than a bet on the future of subprimes.

Three highly sophisticated investors were willing to take the long side of the bet. They were ACA Capital Holdings, a bond insurer who had been deeply involved in subprime investing, IKB Deutsche Industriebank, a Germany-based specialist in mortgage securities, and Goldman itself. ACA also sold a $900 million credit default swap on Abacus for $4 million, which was a bet with very high odds– 225 to one– that Abacus would not default. Since ACA had risked the most on the long side, its wholly owned subsidiary, ACA Management, was given the sole authority to pick every one of the 90 securities in the portfolio. IKB then participated on the long side by buying $150 million worth of Abacas's notes, and Goldman put up the remaining $90 million to complete the financing.

Paulson, the lone short, stood to make $900 million from the ACA credit default swap if he was right about the collapse of subprimes. All four players is this esoteric game had the same data about the 90 underlying securities, but very different opinions about the likelihood of a default. Paulson believed it was a good possibility; ACA, IKB, and Goldman considered this so unlikely they were willing to bet against it at long odds in Abacus. As it turned out, Paulson won the bet.

So where is the fraud? The SEC says Goldman did not fully disclose the history of the deal, including Paulson's role in the creation of Abacus in the prospectus. That is true but ACA knew that its $900 million credit default swap would be paid to the counterparty. It also knew, according to Paulson's top lieutenant in the deal, Paolo Pellegrini, that the counterparty was Paulson. Pellegrini testified to the SEC in 2008 that he had informed ACA Management that Paulson's hedge fund was betting against the transaction. If so, ACA possessed the information that Goldman omitted from the prospects, and went ahead with the deal. And of corse Goldman itself knew. So only one player, IKB bank, which bought Abacus's AAA-rated notes, may not
have known about Paulson's role in Abacus.

In any case, the legal issue here turns on the term "material," which the SEC defines as facts an investor would reasonably want to know before making an investment. The agency contends that Paulson's role in suggesting securities to ACA was "material." The SEC's theory is that Paulson might have "heavily influenced" ACA Management to pick losers for the portfolio. The obvious problem here is that ACA had no reason to succumb to this influence since its corporate parent was risking over $900 million, and therefore had an incentive to pick the safest subprimes possible. As it turned out, not only the subprime securities ACA picked for the portfolio failed, but the vast majority of these securities suffered the same fate, with 99% of them marked down by the rating agencies by the end of 2008. So Abacus would have likely suffered the same fate had ACA picked 90 other such securities. And ACA's losses on Abacus were small change compared to the $21 billion in losses it had in its other subprime funds in which Paulson was not involved.

As Goldman failed to provide what the SEC deemed material information, it settled with the SEC, by paying $550 million in fines and restitutions.

No one can fault the SEC for wanting to restore faith in Wall Street by ferreting
out financial frauds, or penalizing financial banks that failed to disclose material facts. That is its job. But the willingness to transmogrify this hedging device into a deliberate scuttling of a fund that Goldman had invested (and lost) $90 million, reflects the extent that Goldman had become the Giant Vampire Squid in the eyes of the press.

A related charge is that Goldman purposely torpedoed the subprime bubble for its own profit by selling short derivatives in 2007. For example, Michael Lewis, the author of the best-selling *The Big Short*, claimed that Goldman made $10 billion through shorting the residential housing market in 2007. In truth, Goldman was both long and short the market. Its chairman Lloyd Blankfein explained in his testimony that the core of its business is "selling to buyers and buying from sellers." To make money on these transactions, it often offsets long positions that become risky by either selling them or selling derivatives based on them. Whoever buys these instruments from Goldman presumably has a different appreciation of the risk than Goldman. So, in 2007, as prices began to decline, Goldman began offsetting its long position with sales, short sales, and derivatives such as credit default swaps. A Senate subcommittee subsequently asserted that Goldman was short $13.9 billion in residential subprimes in mid 2007. It turned out, however, that the document the subcommittee staff used in this assessment neglected a long position of $5 billion and erroneously mixed in $4.1 billion in commercial real estate. Once this error was corrected, this reduced the number to under $5 billion. Even so, it evidently was not enough to offset the long exposure Goldman had to subprimes in 2007, since instead of making "$10 billion," it had suffered a small loss.

While the practice of selling as well as buying financial instruments bearing on the American mortgage market might seem "disgraceful," as Senator Carl Levin described it, it can also be viewed in the universe of Mammon as an essential means for making price information available to the market. It is the redeeming virtue of greed in a market of ideas. To be sure, in this case, it expressed a negative appreciation of the future of subprimes, which proved correct.

But the effort to expose putative demonic machination went well beyond complaints about short selling. Consider the "mystery man" scenario. After the *New York Times* revealed that a former Goldman financial officer named Dan H. Jester had acted as Treasury Secretary Henry Paulson's "point man" in the $133 billion bailout of AIG, a raft of stories on blogs suggested that Goldman alumni in the Treasury were part of conspiracy. A description of it in *The Huffington Post*, for example, was headlined "How Paulson's People Colluded With Goldman To Destroy AIG, " and pointed out that Treasury Secretary Henry Paulson, who had been CEO at Goldman, had staffed the Treasury with number of ex-Goldman executives, including Jester, who were in contact during the crises with their former colleagues at Goldman. But Paulson's objective was to save, not destroy, AIG. That was also the goal of the Fed and the Government. It was not that AIG itself was too big to fail, but that its trillion dollars in assets were so deeply interwoven into the skein of the global financial system that allowing it to go bankrupt would invite financial Armageddon. For one thing, its subsidiaries operating in 130 countries provided the insurance for a large part of the commerce flowing between China, America, and Europe. If these subsidiaries were to be seized by regulatory authorities as a result of a bankruptcy, world trade might come to a halt, . AIG also held billions of state and municipal funds in its guaranteed investment programs that, if frozen, would paralyze cities throughout America. It would cause an even greater financial meltdown abroad since European banks depended on AIG, through its French subsidiary Banque AIG, to provide the "regulatory capital" that stabilized their mandated capital-to-debt ratios. This notional "capital" was created by complex swaps that would come undone if there was a failure or change of ownership in Banque AIG. Without this capital, Europe's leading banks would be forced to call in their loans. It would also invalidate its credit default swaps which would cause chaos in the debt markets through the globe. In short, AIG was a veritable death star hanging over the world's economy. So the US government had no choice but to step in. In retrospect, it turns out a highly-successful intervention. As of August 2011, the Federal Reserve Bank received all its money back, and the government was repaid nearly $45 billions, and hold 77% of the stock in AIG. After that stock is sold the AIG bailout might wind up costing taxpayers little, if any, money.

As for Goldman itself, the US government made a made a $1.74 billion profit on the assistance it provided it. The Treasury had insisted that it, as well as all the major banks, accept TARP funds to increase their liquidity. It provided it with $10 billion on September 28, 2008, and, as part of the arrangement, Goldman officially became a bank holding company regulated by the New York Federal Reserve Bank. That ended the shadow banking system. Eight months later, Goldman repaid all the TARP funds and what amounted to a staggeringly-high 23 % interest rate. So the Treasury hardly gave Goldman a favorable rate.

The Ahabs of the media will no doubt continue chasing their giant vampire squid, if only, because they believe it there is no end to the wealth it pulls out of the system. In 2010 alone, its earnings of $8.3 billion, resulted in bonuses for many employees of over one million dollars or more at Christmas time. But maximizing profits, despite its negative connotations within the popular culture, is not (yet) a crime.

[2]
The Swiss Gnome Conspiracy

Ten times a year—once a mouth except in August and October—a small elite of well-dressed men arrives in Basel, Switzerland. Carrying overnight bags and attaché cases, they discreetly check into the Euler Hotel, across from the railroad station.

They come to this sleepy city from places as disparate as Tokyo, London, and Washington, D.C., for the regular meeting of the most exclusive, secretive, and powerful supranational club in the world. While here, they are fully serviced by chauffeurs, chefs, guards, messengers, translators, stenographers, secretaries, and researchers. For their relaxation, there is a secluded nearby country club with tennis courts and a swimming pool.

The membership of this club is restricted to a handful of powerful men who determine daily the interest rate, the availability of credit, and the money supply of the banks in their own countries. They include the governors of the U.S. Federal Reserve, the Bank of England, the Bank of Japan, the Swiss National Bank, and the German Bundesbank.

The unabashed purpose of this elite society is to make decisions that aim to influence and, if possible, to control all monetary activities in the industrialized world. The place where this club meets in Basel is a unique financial institution called the Bank for International Settlements—or more simply, the BIS (pronounced "biz" in German).

The BIS was established in May 1930 by a small elite of central bankers to collect and settle Germany's massive World War I reparation payments (hence its name). These lords of finance organized it as a commercial bank with publicly held shares. Their power was such that an international treaty, signed in The Hague in 1930, guaranteed the bank's immunity from government interference, and even taxation, in both peace and war.

Its depositors, the world's central banks, also stored much of their gold there. As the central banks provided it with a profit on every transaction, it required no subsidy from any state, making it truly a supra-government of finance. Congress officially refused to allow the U.S. Federal Reserve to participate in the BIS, or to accept shares in it (which instead were held in trust by the First National City Bank). But the chairman of the Fed quietly slipped over to Basel for important meetings to deal with the financial panics that flared up in Austria, Hungary, Yugoslavia, and Germany in the 1930s, and to prevent the collapse of the global financial system.

These central bankers had to coordinate their rescue efforts in secret, and the meeting spot that provided them with the necessary cover was the BIS, where they regularly went anyway to arrange gold swaps and war-damage settlements. World monetary policy was evidently too important to leave to national politicians. Even during World War II, when the nations, if not their central banks, were belligerents, the BIS continued operating in Basel. The monthly meetings were temporarily suspended in 1944, following Czech accusations that the BIS was laundering gold that the Nazis had stolen from occupied Europe.

After the war, the American government backed a resolution calling for the liquidation of the BIS. The naive idea was that the new International Monetary Fund could take over the BIS' settlement and monetary-clearing functions. What could not be replaced, however, was what existed behind the mask of an international clearing house: a supranational organization for setting and implementing global monetary strategy, which could not be accomplished by a democratic, United Nations-like international agency.

The central bankers, not about to allow anyone to take their club from them, quietly snuffed out the American resolution. Indeed, the BIS grew stronger, and proved particularly useful to the United States in the Cold War years.

When the dollar came under attack in the 1960s, massive swaps of money and gold were arranged at the BIS for the defense of the American currency. It was undeniably ironic that, as the president of the BIS observed, "the United States, which had wanted to kill the BIS, suddenly finds it indispensable."

Up until the late 1970s, the central bankers sought such complete anonymity for their activities that they maintained their headquarters in an abandoned six-story hotel, the Grand et Savoy Hotel Universe, with an annex above the adjacent Frey's Chocolate Shop. Since there purposely was no sign over the door to identify the BIS, visiting central bankers and gold dealers used Frey's, which is across the street from the railroad station, as a convenient landmark.

In the wood-paneled rooms above the shop and hotel, decisions were reached to devalue or defend currencies, to fix the price of gold, to regulate offshore banking, and to raise or lower short-term interest rates. And though the bank shaped a new world order, the public, even in Basel, remained almost totally unaware of its activities.

The BIS had relaxed some this passion for secrecy and, against the better judgment of some of its members, moved to a more efficient eighteen-story cylindrical skyscraper, when I was invited to its headquarters in 1983 by Karl Otto Pohl, who, as president of the German central bank, belonged to the inner club of the BIS. Earlier, I had interviewed Pohl for *Institutional Investor* magazine, and he had complained to me, over a bratwurst-and-beer lunch on the top floor of the Bundesbank in Frankfurt, about the repetitiousness of the meetings he had to attend at the BIS.

"First, there is the meeting on the Gold Pool, then, after lunch, the same faces show up at the G-10. The next day there is the board which excludes the U.S., Japan, and Canada, and then the European Community meeting, which excludes Sweden and Switzerland. But these meetings are not where the real business gets done," he said. That was done at the "inner club" that included Pohl. Since Pohl was telling me about his power, at the end of our leisurely lunch I asked him if he could arrange a visit for me. "Why not," he answered, "You can interview its President Fritz Leutwiler."

When I arrived in Basel the following week, there was no mistaking the BIS' headquarters. Known as the "Tower of Basel" it rose over the medieval city like some misplaced nuclear reactor. I was immediately taken to Dr. Leutwiler's office, which, despite his power, was modest in size. He began the interview by apologizing for the prominence of the bank's new venue: "That was the last thing we wanted. If it had been up to me, it never would have been built."

Despite its irksome visibility, the building has some practical advantages over its predecessor over a chocolate shop, he conceded. For one thing, it is completely air-conditioned and self-contained, with its own nuclear-bomb shelter in the sub-basement, a triply redundant fire-extinguishing system (so outside firemen never have to be called in), a private hospital, and some twenty miles of subterranean archives.

While we talked, his eyes never left the Reuters screen in his office, which signaled currency fluctuations around the globe. He then provided me with a tour of the building. Gunther Schleiminger, the general manager, escorted me around the different levels, and provided a revealing commentary about the layout of one of the financial world's most secretive institutions.

The top floor, with a panoramic view of three countries, Germany, France, and Switzerland, contained a deluxe restaurant, used only to serve the members a buffet dinner on Sunday evenings when they arrive to begin the "Basel weekends."

Aside from those ten occasions, this floor remained ghostly empty. The next three floors down were the suites of offices reserved for the central bankers. On the next floor was the BIS computer, which, for 1983, was state of the art. It was directly linked to the computers of the member central banks and provided instantaneous access to data about the global monetary situation.

On the floor beneath it was the actual bank, where 18 traders, mainly from England and Switzerland, were busy rolling over short-term loans on the Eurodollar markets. They spoke mainly English. Finally, on the lowest floor, gold was being hectically traded.

Traders were constantly on the telephone arranging loans of the bank's gold to international arbitragers, thus allowing central banks to earn interest on gold deposits. Indeed, the BIS is prohibited by its statutes from making anything but short-term loans. So almost all the gold-backed trades were for 30 days.

To back their trades, these traders had roughly one-tenth of the world's gold supply. According to Dr. Leutwiler, the profits the BIS received on this trading had amounted to $162 million the previous year.

But why were the central banks using the BIS to trade their gold? The German Bundesbank, for example, has a superb international trading department and 15,000 employees—at least 20 times as many as the BIS staff. The answer was, of course, secrecy.

By commingling part of their reserves in what amounts to a gigantic mutual fund of short-term investments, the central banks created a convenient screen behind which they can hide their own deposits and withdrawals in financial centers around the world. And the central banks are apparently willing to pay a modest fee to use the cloak of the BIS. They also provided it with a large enough profit to support the other services it provided them.

On paper, the BIS was a small, technical organization with just 86 of its 298 employees ranked as professional staff in 1983. But artfully concealed within this outer shell, like a series of Chinese boxes one inside another, were the operations that truly required the support of the world's central bankers.

The first box inside the bank is the board of directors, drawn from the eight European central banks (England, Switzerland, Germany, Italy, France, Belgium, Sweden, and the Netherlands), which meets on the Tuesday morning of each "Basel weekend."

The board also meets twice a year in Basel with the central banks of other nations. It provides a formal apparatus for dealing with European governments and international bureaucracies like the IMF or the European Economic Community. The board defines the rules and territories of the central banks with the goal of preventing governments from meddling in their purview, including setting the ratio of bank reserves to loans.

To deal with the world at large, there is another Chinese box dealing with the "G-10." This powerful group, which controls most of the transferable money in the world, meets for long sessions on the Monday afternoon of the "Basel weekend."

It is here that broader policy issues, such as interest rates, money-supply growth, economic stimulation (or suppression), and currency rates are discussed.

Directly under the G-10, and catering to all its special needs, is a small unit called the "Monetary and Economic Development

Department," which serves in effect, as its private think tank. This unit produces the occasional blue-bound "economic papers" that provide central bankers from Singapore to Rio de Janeiro, even though they are not BIS members, with a convenient party line.

Finally, there is the inner club, made up of the half dozen or so powerful central bankers. Even when the BIS is not holding a meeting, they are in constant contact with each other by phone. And they all speak the same language when it comes to governments, having shared similar experiences. "Some of us are very old friends," Pohl said, and share the same set of well articulated values about money.

One such value is the firm belief that central banks should act independently of their home governments. A second shared value, according to Pohl, is that politicians should not be trusted to decide the fate of the international monetary system. When Leutwiler became president of the BIS in 1982, he insisted that no government official be allowed to visit during a "Basel weekend." "To be frank," he said, "I have no use for politicians. They lack the judgment of central bankers."

This effectively sums up the common antipathy of the inner club toward "government muddling," as Pohl termed it at our Bundesbank lunch. The other value shared by the inner club is the conviction that when the bell tolls for any single central bank, it tolls for them all. "We are constantly engaged in a balancing act without a safety net," Leutwiler explained.

When Mexico faced bankruptcy in the early 1980s, the issue for the inner club was not the welfare of that country but the stability of the entire banking system. It was clearly an emergency for the inner club. Even though the IMF was prepared to step in, it would require months of paperwork to get approval for the loan, and Mexico needed an immediate $1.85 billion.

After speaking to Miguel Mancera, director of the Banco de Mexico, then-Fed Chairman Paul Volcker called Leutwiler, who was vacationing in the Swiss mountain village of Grison. Leutwiler realized that the entire system was confronted by a financial time bomb. In less than 48 hours, Leutwiler had called the members of the inner club and arranged the temporary bridging loan.

While the loan appeared in the financial press to have come from the BIS, virtually all the funds came from the central banks in the inner club. The BIS merely provided a convenient cloak for the central bankers; Volcker and other members would have to take the political heat individually for what appeared to be the rescue of an underdeveloped country. As Leutwiler told me, with a faint mischievous smile, "Another victory for the Swiss Gnomes."

[3]
The Midas Man

In December 1986, U.S. Attorney Rudolph Giuliani made one of the most extraordinary deals in the annals of American justice. It was with Ivan Boesky, the Wall Street arbitrageur, who inspired the fictional character Gordon Gekko in the movie *Wall Street*. He had admitted using stolen information to make over a $100 million. Not only was he was allowed to plead guilty to a only a single count of securities violations, but he was permitted to keep secret his foreign bank and brokerage accounts, even if they had been enriched by his criminal activity. Similarly, the accounts in his wife and children's name were protected. This accord was not Giuliani's work alone: it was initialed by the U.S. Attorneys in both Washington D.C. and Los Angeles. What Boesky offered to give in return for this leniency was, among other things, information about the secret dealings of a reclusive financier in Los Angeles whose Midas touch had turned junk bonds into gold– Michael Robert Milken.

Even as Giuliani hammered out the final terms of this bargain with Boesky, Milken, on the telephone in his trading room in Beverly Hills, was lining up some $20 billion in financing for raids on such corporate behemoths as US Steel, Gillette, and Trans World Corporation. Despite the scope of his operations, he had tried to remain invisible to the world at large by denying all press interviews, avoiding social functions and buying up photographs of himself.

Now, with a stroke of the pen by Boesky and three U.S. Attorneys, Milken was suddenly in the cross-hairs of a highly-visible federal investigation.

Despite this new focus on his activities, and rumors that his indictment was imminent, Milken bravely appeared in Beverly Hills Hilton Ballroom, for his ninth-- and last junk bond convention in April. He walked amid four bodyguards, wearing a beige sports suit and defiant red tie. His Californian sun tan and toothy grin made him look much more boyish than his forty-one years. So did the well-fitting hair piece he wore. The hereditary loss of hair he suffered as a teen added to his painful shyness-- and reclusiveness from the press.

More than 2000 clients of Milken's had shown up-- many, for no other reason, than to show their support for him. They were mainly middle-level money managers from Life insurers, Savings and Loans Associations, Pension funds, College Endowments, off-shore banks, mutual funds, financial syndicates and other institution investors. Over the past decade they had invested scores of billions of dollars in his junk bonds. Many owed their performance record, if not their careers to him. Even if they had heard his mesmerizing message before--and pointed jokes-- they watched him intently.

Milken flashed a quick smile the audience-- as if to say the world was still under control. But there was also a jarring twist in his face-- suggesting the enormous strain he was under. As he began his lilting, almost preachy cadence, his deep set eyes grew more intense. Like some leader at a revival meeting, he looked dead ahead, making sure he was in total control of his audience.

"We should all recognize from the moment we wake up in the morning, we don't like change. We don't like it when our children stop listening to Mary Poppins and all of a sudden have a rock video blasting in the house...we don't like it when they change their hairdo or dress. People who run corporations don't like change either."

He hesitated a moment for effect; a grimace on his face-- as if he could personally feel the pain these "people" were in. As everyone in the room fully realized, the staggering change he was talking about was the one he himself had brought about-- the junk bond revolution.

"One way to insulate yourself is to deny change is occurring. You lash out at people, and whose easiest to lash out at...Wall Street."

He is thin body was suddenly taut with nervous energy. He looked at his supporters, who knew that he was explaining, in his own code, why the government was about to come crashing down on him.

"Much of American business has run to the [government] and said, 'Let's change the rules, we don't want competition, we don't want pressure....Where the corporate officer has denied the market place its right of judgment, and put up barriers to change... and become an ostrich, eventually change becomes violent."

Milken left the conference mobbed by supporters. Just as they had put their faith in his new bonds-- and profited by doing so-- they accepted his message: the establishment was after him because they feared change. As one supporter stated, "corporate America is hoping to indict Mike Milken...so it can go back to sleep for another 30 years." It was, to them part of "the war" on Wall Street.

Whatever the reason for the powerful reaction against Milken, one thing was certain: he was no ordinary financier. In a few short years, he had reshaped the financial world in a way that no one else had done since J.P. Morgan in the nineteenth century. What he did almost single-handily was destroy the dam of traditional restraints that had effectively penned in a half-trillion dollar reservoir of capital. When this pool of funds, known as the bond market, which had been retained for more than a century as the private fishing pond for Fortune 500 and utility companies, suddenly was channeled by Milken into new hands-- including non-traditional entrepreneurs and corporate raiders-- it changed not only existing relations on Wall Street but the hold of management over publically-held corporations. For better or worse, it threatened to irreversibly alter the balance of power in corporate America. How one man, an outsider without any connections, could bring about changes of this magnitude, and make perhaps a billion dollars for himself in the process, is a story of American capitalism.

Only a decade earlier, Milken was getting his business degree from the Wharton School. Now, he was the central figure in a struggle for control of a vast part of the corporate wealth of America. "I never saw myself as a revolutionary...all the revolutionaries I know are dead," he told me.

What Milken had sought throughout his remarkable rise to power, he explained, was not chaos-- but control over the things around him. "I don't like it when they change my seat at work, it probably disorients me for a week," he explained. When he moved his 20 man bond trading department from New York to Los Angeles in 1978, he found, when he sat at the center of the new X-shaped trading desk he found it difficult to see the two employees on the corners of the desk. He stormed out of the office, ordering the entire office to be redesigned so that he could see everyone from his seating, at all times. Subsequently, he moved his trading room to the building that houses Gump's on Wilshire Boulevard-- a building that he, and his partners, own. "I have no private office," he said to me, "I never had one in my life."

Ever since he had been a teenager in the San Fernando Valley Milken found one means of getting control was simply working longer hours than anyone else. At high school he was both head cheerleader and Prom Chairman, and earned money for himself working nights at a diner. At Berkeley, he made Phi Beta Kappa while moonlighting at the accounting firm of Touche Ross. He then enrolled at Wharton, where he commuted on a greyhound bus from Philadelphia to New York to trade bonds at Drexel. He told Frederick Joseph, who is now CEO of Drexel, "I don't know if I am smarter than anyone else but I can work 25 per cent harder."

He undertook, as a matter of routine, to work a fifteen hour day. He usually arrives at the trading room at 4:30 a.m.-- toting two dog-eared canvas bags full of reports and memos that he had taken home to read-- and remains there until at least 7:30 at night. "Lunch," usually a sandwich and soda, is brought in on a tray for him, and everyone else, at 10 a.m. He neither smokes or drinks-- not even coffee, explaining, "I don't need stimulants." Three assistants, who work in relays, starting at 4 a.m., try to keep up with him.

He uses the telephone as another means of extending his control. As young women in jeans move around the trading room passing scribbled notes to him, he relentlessly phones clients to tell them the "story" on companies whose bonds he is "placing." His pitch is often in the form of long monologues.

Keeping visitors waiting for audiences is another means of maintaining control. Not uncommonly, corporate executives begin cuing up in the conference rooms outside from early in the morning to late at night. They come typically to discuss borrowing money for their company in the junk bond market. Often, they then wait for over an hour. When Milken finally strides into the room, he is accompanied by a host of his aides, relevant financial experts and executives from Drexel's corporate finance department. There are, not uncommonly, more than twenty people sitting around the oval-shaped table.

According to executives who have gone through such "audiences," Milken usually listens patiently and courteously to their case for getting access to junk bond financing. He then, in another act of control, dismisses from the room all but four or five participants. In this smaller group, he then presents his own analysis of, and strategy for, the company seeking money in the bond market. One industrialist who sat through such an audience was "stunned" as he described it afterwards, by Milken's intimate knowledge of his company's financial situation. Then, suddenly, the audiences would be over and Milken would disappear back into the trading room.

Nominally, Milken is merely a minor executive at Drexel--the vice president in charge of its Beverly Hills branch office. In fact, in an extraordinary arrangement, he operates what is tantamount to a company within a company. By moving his staff to LA, he was able to operate outside of the sort of direct supervision that he might have to contend with in N.Y. His inner circle includes Lowell Milken, his younger brother and a lawyer by training, Peter Ackerman, his right-hand man and a Fletcher School Ph.D. and Richard Sandler-- his personal lawyer. He also has his own accountants and consultants. He also takes a large part of Drexel's profit: In 1986 alone, he, and his staff, reportedly got over a quarter billion dollars in bonuses-- much of which was invested in Milken's extramural ventures-- and highly-aggressive tax-shelters. In these investments, he has made many of these top aides multi-millionaires in their own rights and partners of his.

Milken's position proceeded directly from his domination over junk bonds. Once considered something of a joke on Wall Street, they become by the mid-1980s, under Milken's direction, the main means of financing through debt the expansion of medium sized corporations-- which meant 95% of the corporations in America. Although he had no exclusive monopoly on junk bonds, his ability to sell them to financial institutions, through his personal network of money managers, made him one of the most powerful financiers in the world.

How Milken created this new universe of money in a few short years, with himself at the center as the "grand sorcerer" of finance, as the Institutional Investor called him, is remarkable testimony to the power of a single idea. The insight came to him gradually in the mid seventies, he explained. He then was working at Drexel in New York as a specialist in so-called "fallen angels"-- which were the bonds of once great corporations that, because they had fallen from grace, had been downgraded by the rating services from investment quality (BB or better) to "junk." His job, figuring out whether the actual risks of them defaulting was outweighed by the premium interest they paid, led him to question the structure of the entire market for capital in the United States.

When he recounted his thinking on how the corporate economy gets its money, "The World According to Milken," as he put it-- he reminded me of the chess prodigy Bobby Fischer. Just as Fischer could see combinations in a chess board no one else could, Milken seemed to see moves not obvious to others in finance. With a series of assertions, often in incomplete verbal shorthand, he would move from level to level.

Level One. "What is a bank?" he asked rhetorically. "It is nothing more than a bunch of loans."

Level two. " How safe are these loans?" "They are made mainly to three groups that may never repay them in a real economic crisis-- home owners, farmers and consumers of big ticket items."

Level Three. "What guarantees these loans?" "These banks usually have $100 in loans for every dollar of equity-- which means there is very little backing them up."

Level Four. "They are hardly a risk-free investment yet their bonds get triple-A ratings" " What does this tell us about bond ratings?"

This brought him to his main target: the bond rating system. As it had existed for a hundred years, two companies-- Standard & Poor's and Moody's-- assigned corporate bonds a letter grade rating descending from AAA to C. Anything above BB was considered investment-grade, which meant there was virtually no risk of default, and the bond-buyer could count on a fixed rate of interest. Since the rating was awarded on the basis of how large the company was, as well as its historical stability, Milken found only "the 600 to 700 largest companies qualified." These were companies with assets over $200 million, and which had been in business for decades. Because of the rating system, they were the only companies in which many insurance companies, pension plans, college endowments, banks and other institutions permitted their money-managers to buy bonds. This "half-trillion-dollar capital market", as Milken calculated it, was closed to the other "24,000 American corporations." These excluded companies could only borrow from commercial banks, at unpredictable short-term interest rates, or from insurance companies, which attached restrictive covenants to the money.

This "black and white" distinctions made no sense to Milken. As he saw it from his analysis of "fallen angels," the underlying "risk free" premise was wrong: "There is no such thing as a risk free investment." Top rated bonds could fall precipitously in value, not only if the company went bankrupt, but if its credit-rating was lowered because their industry declined-- like steel and ship-building did in the seventies. Ratings measured "the past not the future" risk. "This was crazy." Milken said "rating services had the wrong computer program."

To correctly weigh the risks, it was necessary to appraise the future. He reasoned: "The value of a company is the sum of two components: its past, as represented by its historic balance sheet, and its future, represented by its prospects." By concentrating on the first component in his equation--the historical balance sheet-- the rating services had seriously neglected the other component--future cash flow.

"And that what bonds are all about-- getting paid off in the future," he added. He cited the case of Metromedia-- which then owned four television stations. "You didn't have to know much about its past record, or the number of years it paid a dividend, or what letter the rating services gave it. All one had to do was be able to add together four numbers-- the value of its stations in New York, L.A., Chicago and Boston-- to find the total value greatly exceeded what it owed." So long as one believed these stations would not decrease in value in the foreseeable future, its bonds would be a safe investment "whatever their ratings."

This brought Milken to the next level of his insight. If bonds were pegged to their future cash flow, rather than past track record, then the old rules would no longer hold. Nor would the investment-grade labels matter. Bonds would then become, like common stock and real estate, just another form of risk management, which is what Milken saw them to be in reality. If the bonds of medium-sized companies were more risky, they could compensate the buyer for the extra gamble by paying extra interest. He assumed that many growth companies could afford to pay this premium interest out of their future earnings (especially since interest, unlike dividends on stocks, is tax deductible).

What he eventually came up with was a cross between a bond and a common stock. It was called a bond, and therefore institutions, restricted to bonds, could buy it for their portfolios, but, in paying out a large slice of its future cash flow to the holder, it acted like stock. Unlike existing junk bonds, which were the debris of fallen companies, Milken custom designed his issues to be unrated bonds. He realized they were "subversive" since they undercut the established rating system, but, as an outsider, this did not disturb him. He had always been, as he described himself, "something of an iconoclast." He, moreover, saw that if he could open up the huge capital market to growth corporations, they would beat a path to his door. Milken conceived of his role as a marriage-broker, "bringing about kind of a marriage between institutions" and aggressive-new corporations.

At Drexel, Milken had already proven himself a money-making phenomena. By 1976, he was earning over 100 per cent on the capital he was given to trade his exotic Fallen Angels -- and got a $5 million bonus (which he immediately re-invested). When Fred Joseph listened to his analyses, he realized that Milken, "understood credit better than anyone else in the country." Joseph then headed Drexel's corporate finance department, which would have to work in close collaboration with Milken in selecting and advising corporations that issued these new bonds. But the profits would be enormous-- if Milken could persuade money-managers of the validity of his concept, and thereby break the strangle-hold the rating services had on the bond market.

The idea required changing the mind set of institutions. Even if it meant earning higher returns, money managers had, as Milken shrewdly recognized, "career reasons" for sticking to buying bonds that carried an investment-grade rating. As long as they bought bonds with this "seal of approval," their careers would not be in jeopardy-- even if the bonds went bankrupt (as, for example, the Washington State Bonds did). On the other hand, if they invested their funds' money in anything else, they would be held personally accountable.

Milken therefore embarked on a determined campaign to bring the more aggressive money managers into an alliance with him. Like any political campaign aimed at changing perceptions, Milken's crusade operated at different levels; public, and hidden.

As if to symbolize his break with the establishment, he moved his headquarters from Wall Street to Los Angeles on July 4th 1978. It was his 32nd birthday-- and his declaration of personal independence from New York. His first order of business was, he recalled teaching his top aides "how to communicate ideas."

His immediate target were the money-managers who invested the portfolio of the highly-competitive thrift banks, pension funds and life insurers. Since the very survival of these institutions, unlike older and more established ones in the East, depended on their being able to attract new clients by paying the highest possible rates of return. They desperately needed some edge over rivals that put their funds only in investment-grade bonds; and Milken offered them the means to save themselves: junk bonds. They still had to be convinced these new instruments were safe.

Milken worked tirelessly to tell them the message what they wanted to hear: ratings were irrational. In his pitch, he compared rating services to movie reviewers that gave theater owners "incorrect reviews" of risks-- with the result that the theaters missed booking the right films. He argued that they ignored the growth potential in their equation. After he laid down the logic of junk bonds, he ran through numbers intended to demonstrate how the higher interest would more than compensate for any losses through defaults in a portfolio of junk bonds. The "bottom line" was that they could earn more money than their competitors in the world of institutional finance. It was a message his audiences evidently wanted to hear.

In a remarkably short period of time, Milken won over a host of money managers with "billion dollar checks in their pocket." As these money managers found junk bonds gave them an edge of over five percent over investment grade bonds-- or $50 million a year for every billion they had in their institution's portfolio-- they were able to attract more institutions to their funds. Other money managers, seeing the results, joined the ranks of the converted.

Many of these fund managers whom I saw, not only accepted his philosophy-- but preached it themselves. Howard Marks, the managing director of Trustco, a Beverly Hills based manager of pension funds, for example, had been convinced by Milken about the bias in the rating system when he was at Citibank in 1977. He recalled Milken talked then not only about making money but, on a more altruistic level, about how the nation would benefit by making capital available to growth companies. He then moved to Trust Company of the West, which invests pension funds; and by investing 1.5 billion in junk bonds, he became one of the top fund managers in America. (He also has been recruited by Milken to help him coach a children's basketball team.)

The story was the same with Thomas Spiegel. When Milken met him, his family owned a small thrift, Columbia Savings and Loan, which invested its funds mainly in government-backed 30 year mortgages. As short-term interest rate steadily rose in the 1970s, S&Ls had to pay progressively higher rates to get the public to buy their Certificates of Deposits, which drove many to the brink of bankruptcy. Milken showed Spiegel that the answer lay in substituting higher-yielding junk bonds for mortgages in its portfolio. By doing this, Spiegel had increased his bank's assets from 400 million to 4 billion dollars-- much of it invested in Milken's bonds.

As the number of converts grew, Milken created an annual jamboree for them in Beverly Hills. As part of the logistics, he hired fleets of stretch limos to shuttle the money managers around; plush restaurants, such as Chasen's, to wine and dine them, and entertainers, such as Frank Sinatra, Diana Ross and Kenny Rogers to amuse them. For his more exclusive clients, there were also stag parties in bungalow Eight of the Beverly Hills Hotel. As one participant, who attended in 1985, recalls, about 20 "starlets" were ushered into the room, like " pigeons brought in a net to a skeet shoot-- and then let loose for the guests to shoot at." The "starlets" were arranged through a model agency partly owned by one of his business associates. There was even a plan to charter the Concorde for a supersonic outing to Wimbledon, where Milken's top clients would have their own tennis clinic with Virginia Wade.

But despite such excursions, the purpose of these multi-million dollar conferences was, as Milken explained it, to give junk bond buyers "a sense of purpose." Beginning at 6 a.m, there were presentations by corporations that were issuing these bonds, followed by "news breaks" by Milken, where he acted as both a MC and cheerleader.

Among these carefully orchestrated events were sessions in which speakers stressed the good junk bonds were doing for the economy. For example, in 1985, first, Senator Chick Hecht told how the country needed growth companies, then a series of economists explained how junk bonds were crucial to growth companies, followed by Ralph M. Ingersoll, the CEO of Ingersoll Newspapers, who told how they had made his company more productive. Finally, to unrestrained cheers, Milken summed up the message.

The change he had brought about through his crusade was that the 2000 or so money managers in the audience were no longer limited in the bonds they bought to a few hundred investment-grade companies; they could buy bonds in thousands of unrated companies. He had opened up a new universe of speculation to them.

Milken accomplished this feat not through his skill as a bond trader but through his skills as a salesman. He was Wall Street's version of the Pied Piper-- leading wayward fund managers from their traditional village. The main occupation of his "traders" was selling bonds to his long list of institutional customers, which they "distributed" according to his instructions-- though they also bought and sold bonds to support the market (and made the spread). The bulk of the profit he generated for Drexel came not from any sort of arbitrage between junk bonds and investment grade bonds-- which, as he explained it to me, he never really did-- but from the fees he got from selling previously unsalable corporate debt.

These money-managers were willing to go along with Milken not solely because of his mesmerizing presentations-- though they provided the "doing good" rationale their superiors might like to hear-- but because of the track record of his junk bonds. The companies he financed boomed, rather than defaulted. In 1986, for example, not a single one of his companies missed an interest payment. He also provided them with a liquid market in which they could quickly sell any junk bonds that made them nervous. Moreover, the prices for these bonds, despite fluctuations in other markets, moved very little. This established what appeared to be a very stable, as well as profitable, medium for the institutional funds that they had been entrusted with investing.

The means by which Milken maintained the appearance of a stable junk bond market was a far less visible part of his strategy. From the moment he moved to California, aside from giving his pitch to money managers, he sought out alliances with larger financiers who personally controlled other financial companies-- especially insurers with large portfolios of bonds. Among the allies he made were Saul Steinberg (Reliance Group Insurers); Fred Carr (First Executive Life Insurance), Carl Lindner (American Financial Corporation), and the Belzberg Brothers (First National Corporation). Milken's relations with these financiers went beyond merely selling them bonds. In the case of some, such as Carr and Steinberg, he became their partner in other joint ventures. He also acted as their financier when they need to raise their own money to acquire other companies. What he created was a common set of interests between himself and others controlling financial companies. Fred Carr's First Executive alone invested most of its 1.4 billion dollar portfolio in junk bonds (as well as setting up an offshore re-insurance company, First Stratford, in partnership with Milken. The extent to which he depended on a handful of financiers was revealed by Milken in a deposition he gave in a law suit involving the Green Tree Acceptance Corporation. He acknowledged that "I would not consider it unusual to find six or seven institutions buying anywhere from 50 to 70 per cent" of his junk bonds.

Moreover, Milken, together with present and former Drexel employees, became a heavy investor in his own junk bonds. The resources at his disposal included, among other entities, his personal trading account, estimated to be over 150 million dollars, the Milken family foundation (which in 1984 reported buying $104,621, 379 worth of securities) and a half-dozen partnerships, he had organized with his employees, some dating back to the mid-1970s, in which they re-invested much of the profits and bonuses they had receive at Drexel.

In addition, Milken, with a few top aides, had a controlling interest in First Stratford, the off-shore re-insurance company, which had 734 million dollars in assets .Milken was also a partner in two investment vehicles run by his former trading assistants-- Bass Limited Investment Partnerships, with two billion dollars in assets; and Pacific Asset Holding, run by his former chief aide, Gary Winnick (who himself invested $30 million), which engages in everything from risk arbitrage of take over stocks to Leveraged Buy Outs. It reportedly has a billion dollars in capital with which to trade junk bonds.   Offshore in Bermuda, along with First Stratford, there is Garrison Investments, operated by still another of his former aides, Guy Dove III. It reportedly re-invests over three billion dollars in municipal holdings, pension plan and other institutional funds-- much of it in junk bonds.

Finally, Milken also has a powerful voice in Drexel's own $3 billion bond portfolio, if not total control. He is its third largest share holder-- after Bank Lambert in Brussels and its own pension plan. According to estimates of former associates of Milken, all these funds-- either controlled by Milken, his former aides or Drexel, may be as much as 10 billion dollars. If effectively traded back and forth between issues, this sum could do much to create the image of a stable market.

Milken thus became, aside from a bond salesman, a market maker for all junk bonds. His Beverly Hills office did, according to a deposition he gave, 250,000 transactions a month. Within this system, money was commonly moved from one coded account to another without the name of the buyer or seller being identified, even to his own employees. "He didn't respect any conventional boundaries," an arbitrageur, who knew Milken well, observed. "It all may have been out of control," a competitor at Morgan Stanley suggested. On the other hand, such formulations, based on orthodox precepts about bond trading, may have seriously underestimated the leverage over the market that wasn't visible to outsiders. With billions of dollars flowing through his various entities, and acting himself, under different hats, as buyer, seller, market-maker and investment banker, Milken had an extraordinary tight grip not only over the prices of bonds in his market-- but over the perception of the entire phenomena.

By 1986, the small stream of money he had diverted from the investment-grade market in the late 1970s quickly turned into a torrential river of funds. Entire industries, such as cable television, health care and regional airlines were developed through the proceeds. And it nurtured a whole new class of entrepreneurs-- men like Henry B. Kravis, who, through his firm, Kohlberg, Kravis Roberts, organized over $30 billion in leveraged buy outs; Rupert Murdoch, who through his "fourth network" and other innovations, forged a global media empire; William McGowan, who, through MCI, built a competing phone system to ATT, Ted Turner, who developed 24 hour cable news and Frank Lorenzo, who, through competition and mergers, created the largest airline in the United States.

If this new source of financing had only been used for helping medium size companies, the corporate establishment might have more easily accepted it. But as it poured in at an accelerated rate, Milken, and his associates at Drexel, began using it to finance corporate raiders, such as Carl Icahn, Ronald Perlman and T. Boone Pickens. Up until the junk bond market became available, few financiers could borrow sufficient capital to get control of multibillion dollar corporations. Now A single client of Milken's, Perlman, who had already taken over Revlon, was now bidding $9 billion for three different companies. Icahn, who had taken over TWA, and going after US Steel, compared management to "gardeners" who had come to think they had owned the estates were paid to take care of." Pickens, who had attacked some of the largest oil companies in the world--including Gulf, Phillips and Uncial-- was now spearheading a political movement, the United Shareholders of America, to fight the "corpocracy." All three raiders were seen, for good reason, as "Milken's creations." These raids-- and the leveraged buy outs and restructuring they led to-- rapidly began to change the balance between owners and managers.

Milken pointed out that whereas the entrepreneurs using his junk-bonds owned 30% of their companies, the managers (and Directors) of "Corporate America" owned less than 1% of their company. This swing in the "delicate balance" between entrepreneurial and managerial companies was causing "some pain," as he put it. Although he conceded it "was unfair to blame the manager if the owner had not showed up for 30 years"; now, through his junk bonds, they were showing up. As leader of the junk bond movement, he had to rationalize what was happening in terms of "doing good."

He spoke of the conflict was between value and size. Owners sought the former. They wanted to see the value of their investment increase, even if it meant reducing the size of the overall company by selling divisions that they couldn't themselves manage efficiently to others. The example, he gave was the new owners of Beatrice, who sold its coca cola bottling plant back to Coke, and its Playtex division back to its original founder, increased the value of their investment by over a billion dollars but reduced the size of the conglomerate. Managers, on the other hand, tended to be concerned with the size of their domain, which, in many cases, defined their standing in the community. Milken argued this focus often led to inefficient, citing in the case of Beatrice, that the previous management had spent over 100 million dollars sponsoring auto races, which they evidently personally enjoyed, and for an advertising campaign to create a corporate image for Beatrice-- though none of its products were sold under the Beatrice brand.

The idea that values could be increased by reducing the size of corporations provided an appealing logic for financing takeovers. If the new owners could increase the cash flow by selling off parts of the company, this increment could be committed to repaying the bonds. Moreover, to make this takeover financing less risky, Milken arranged the transaction so that the bonds were only bought when, and if, the raider acquired control of the company. In addition, in case the deal failed to come to fruition-- as most did-- they buyers-in-waiting received a handsome "commitment fee" from the raider. Institutions, seeing a profit with a minimum apparent risk, rushed in to provide this take over financing. (The American Lutheran Church' pension, for example, received a $750,000 commitment fee for agreeing to be a buyer-in-waiting of 10 millions dollars of bonds, without putting up any money). These pledges which Milken lined up allowed Drexel to provide raiders with a letter stating it was "highly confident" the financing could be arranged. For its part, Drexel received a cut of the "commitment fees"-- which rarely involved anything more than a promise -- which amounted to hundreds of millions of dollars.

In terms of sheer power, Milken was reached his zenith in the fall of 1986. Over 900 companies had become issuers of junk bonds -- which was larger than the number of companies issuing investment-grade bonds, and the junk bond market was channeling up to four billion dollars a month to companies excluded from the traditional bond market. Because of Milken's money machine, corporations signed on with Drexel (whether they needed the money-- or out of feared, if they didn't, Drexel would supply the money to their competitor). Drexel, which had been a minor brokerage house 5 years earlier, now, in terms of profit, had become America's leading investment bank. Drexel's pre-tax profits were reportedly over $1.5 billion in 1986.

Suddenly, as Business Week warned on its cover, no one was safe anymore. Felix Rohatyn, a senior partner in Lazard Frere, warned "The takeover game as it is practiced today is really a little like the arms race. You have to stop it before it gets out of control." Lane Kirkland, the President of the AFL-CIO, called it "an outrage and a bloody scandal." Senator William Proxmire, a Democrat from Wisconsin, stated "The rising tide of hostile takeovers threatens the foundation of the American business system."

Sir James Goldsmith, who has been both a client and an opponent of Milken's, saw the conflict proceeding from the threat to take power away from those who had held it. "I don't know whether or not Mike Milken realized at the time that he had found a way of financing an immense revolution in America, but now he has witnessed the full power of the establishment triangle: big business, big unions and big government." He then added, " As I European, I witnessed the same alliance trying to avoid change and neutralizing those responsible for it."

"It is nothing short of war," declared one of America's leading industrialists, who asked not to be identified out of fear of being caught in the cross-fire.

Wall Street was only one front in this war. It was fought also in court rooms, board rooms and back rooms of state legislatures, as well as on television and op pages, where accusations were made that corporate managers were "corpocrats," and raiders "assassins in three piece suits." It was even waged on the streets of Akron, Ohio, were Goodyear organized workers, wearing rubber face masks, to march in protest against Sir James Goldsmith.

At the center of the conflict was an almost philosophic disputation about the purpose of the large corporation in the scheme of American capitalism. In one camp, the defenders of the present system of corporate stewardship, argue that the corporation must be regarded not just as a private profit-making but as a public institution. As such, they must serve not only their legal owners--the share-holders-- but broader interests, including their workers, suppliers, the local community and the nation. They hold that management, which represents these community interests as well as shareholders, is best suited to run these institutions.

In the other camp, the raiders and their allies, argue that corporation best serve others by serving their legal owners-- the shareholders. In this view, they benefit other constituencies--such as labor, suppliers and communities-- not by being charitable institutions but by making the most efficient use of their resources-- which may mean selling or closing down unproductive divisions. They hold that only managers who are accountable to owners have the incentive to make such hard choices. Such accountability comes down to owners having the ability to fire them-- which may mean taking over the corporation.

Behind these different rationales (which belligerents may-- or may not-- sincerely believe), both sides are after the same prize: control of the corporate wealth of America. The means for waging this battle is money.

By opening up the capital market, like some Aladdin's cave, to outsiders, Milken has made himself central to this war. To end the threat to take away their stewardship, and power, corporate managers had to somehow close the cave. No unrated bonds, no take overs.

Under siege, corporate managements turned in increasing numbers to State and Federal government for help. By November 1986, some 30 bills had been proposed in Congress, while a dozen states passed or considered anti-take over laws. With the Business Round Table, which represents the Fortune 500, warning that junk bond take overs could bring on a 1929-type depression, the Federal Reserve Bank raised margin requirements on junk bond financing, State Insurance

Commissions mandated reduced investment in junk bonds, and Congressmen called for new restrictions on their purchase.

Milken tried to explain these attacks on his junk bond empire to money-managers with a baseball metaphor. "Just imagine there was a baseball team, like the N.Y. Yankees, that won all the time. It even came to believe it had a divine right to win. Then a new team came along whose pitchers knew how to throw curve balls and sliders which its hitters couldn't hit. It began to lose. So its manager decided, rather than teaching them how to hit these pitches, to go to the Commission -- and have them banned."

Senators on the Banking Committee listened, the Chairman, William Proxmire, opened a special hearing on Wall Street by asking "How much do we really know about the corporate takeover game and the complex network of information that circulates among investment bankers, takeover lawyers, corporate raiders, arbitragers, stock brokers, junk bond investors and public relations specialists?"

This question, which raised the specter of finding a vast criminal conspiracy behind the battle for corporate control, was directed to Rudolph Giuliani, a prosecutor who had made his reputation proving criminal conspiracies against the Mafia, and Gary Lynch, the Director of the SEC's enforcement division. Senator Proxmire explained that in 1933, the same Senate Banking Committee had "recruited" a young attorney named Ferdinand Pecora to go after "white collar criminals" on Wall Street. Pecora, as the Senate's chosen instrument, went after the villain of that era: The House of Morgan-- who had turned the nation's capital markets into a private preserve.

The Chairman then came to his point: "Mr. Giuliani and Mr. Lynch, you are the Ferdinand Pecoras of the 1980s; through your vigilance, Wall Street is being rid of some of its criminals whose greed has cut a sorry path through our American system." His message--and charge-- was clear. The new Pecoras' target would be Mike Milken, who ironically was responsible for breaching the walls around J.P. Morgan's preserve.

Giuliani had already cut his deal with Boesky. He also cut deals with the seven other participants in the Boesky ring (who worked for such firms as Lazard Frere, Shearson, Wachtell Lipton, Kidder Peabody and Drexel)-- thus ending the case with 8 guilty pleas. The New Pecora abruptly shifted his investigative focus from the inside-trading scam to possible irregularities in Mike Milken's operation.

Giuliani suggested the tough tactics he planned to employ when he was asked what he believed was the difference between culprits in organized crime and those on Wall Street. He answered the latter "roll easier"-- meaning that Wall Street financiers, when threatened with doing hard-time in prison, could be more easily induced to implicate others to save themselves. To this end, he arrested Timothy Tabor, who had worked in the Kidder Peabody Arbitrage Department, too late in the afternoon for him to arrange bail-- or even a lawyer. No indictment had been obtained, nor was he ever advised he was being investigated. He was then told he would have to spend the night in prison if he did not cooperate with Giuliani's investigation by making a taped phone call to his ex-boss. Giuliani candidly explained "This isn't an invitation to a tea party-- people are arrested in the hope they will tell you everything that happened." (In this case , Tabor proved an exception to Giuliani's prediction and, rather than "cooperating" spent the night in jail. (Giuliani subsequently dropped these charges when it came time for him to have a day in court).

Parking violations, as the name implies, involves a brokerage house or bank keeping a client's stock in its own name in disregard of its reporting requirements. Such "parking" may allow the client to temporarily bypass his margin requirements, keep secret his position in a company that otherwise he would have to disclose, or stay within limits imposed by other rules. It may also sometimes used by portfolio managers who "window dress" their fund's holdings for public reporting purposes. Such infractions of the myriad of reporting requirements was not a rare occurrence. As one Wall Street executive observed,"There is not a firm on Wall Street that can be sure it has not, at one time or another, committed some technical violation of these laws." Although clearly a breach of the securities law, up until now no one ever went to prison for such an infraction.

The "new Pecoras" have, according to their testimony, a very different idea about "parking violations." They then subpoenaed numerous Drexel employees and gradually built a case not only against Milken but against his family.

It was a war Milken could not win. As his lawyer later noted, "Milken's biggest problem was that some of his most ingenious but entirely lawful maneuvers were viewed, by those who initially did not understand them, as felonious, precisely because they were novel – and often extremely profitable." But some of the more complex maneuvers, depending on how his clients used them, could also be violations of the law. The RICO laws had been designed to battle the Mafia, and up until 1989, it had been almost exclusively used against alleged members of organized crime. But in March 1989, the government used it as a weapon against Milken, indicting him on scores of separate counts of "racketeeering." Even if he could win acquittal on all these 98 counts, dozens of State Attorney-General had plans to move against him. His brother, mother, and family foundation would also face indictment or legal actions . In April 1990, Milken decided it was a legal battle he could not pursue, and agreed to plead guilty to six counts. Five involved infractions of the law involving helping clients conceal their identity or tax liability. The sixth was conspiring with these clients to commit these crimes. None involved inside trading or fraud against his clients. The total injury from these crimes, according to the Judge's reckoning was $318,000. Milken was sentenced to 10 years in prison and fined $200 million. He then paid another $900 million to settle all the civil litigation against him and his family. His sentence was later reduced to two years– and he served 22 months.

No sooner did he get out of prison than he got a possible death sentence in the form of prostate cancer. In 1993, he sought out experimental state of the art treatments, which were not only successful for him but led him to create the Prostate Cancer Foundation.

In retrospect, Milken changed the financial world in a way that no one else had done since J.P. Morgan. By destroying the dam of traditional restraints that had effectively penned in huge a reservoir of capital in a highly-restricted bond market, he helped channel vast amounts of capital into new hands and provide entrepreneurs, especially those with novel technologies.

[4]

Pied Piper of Yale

 David Swensen pioneered "alternative investment strategy," which led many university endowment funds to pour over one hundred billion of dollars into illiquid investments by the crash of 2008. Swensen achieved his almost guru status as Yale's chief investment officer, which he became in 1985. A PhD in economics and lecturer in finance, Swensen achieved such consistently high returns for Yale's endowment fund until 2009 that the strategy, which he outlined in his 2000 book *Pioneering Portfolio Management: An Unconventional Approach to Institutional Investment*, was widely imitated by other university endowment funds. Indeed, by 2008, it was difficult to find a major university that was not dancing to Swensen's tune and, for all practical purposes, it replaced the traditional strategy of dividing a portfolio mainly between blue-chip bonds and equities.

The heart of his strategy is to reduce drastically the allocation for bonds, equities, and cash, and substitute for them a portfolio of illiquid investments that included participation in leveraged buyouts, hedge funds, and stockpiles of physical assets. Swensen argued in his book that such illiquid investments carry less risk and more potential for high returns than stocks or bonds. His position is that because endowment funds do not have to concern themselves with withdrawals for taxes or redemptions to their investors, they do not need the liquidity of the major stock and bond markets and can therefore avoid losses from short-term fluctuations.

Swensen's most persuasive point up until 2008 was his own remarkable performance at Yale. By 2000, he had put most of its endowment fund in illiquid investments. While high-flying U.S. stocks collapsed in the Internet bubble in 2000-01, Yale's endowment fund made money as its assets rose in value, and it outperformed almost every other major endowment fund—many of which lost money—as its president, Richard Levin, pointed out. In short order, all of the Ivy League schools, including Harvard, with the world's largest endowment, had moved their portfolios into alternative investments. By 2008, these universities had also, as the price of entry into private-equity, made unfunded commitments to add capital equal to slightly more than 25 percent of their entire endowment fund, when and if called upon to do so by the fund managers.

How illiquid were these alternative investments? Consider, for example, the private-equity funds in which these universities became limited partners to participate in leveraged buyouts and other such deals. The general partners, which were private-equity houses such as KKR, typically required that endowment funds make a commitment of as long as ten years to not withdraw their investment. They often also required a commitment to furnish additional funds in the response to their "capital call." If all went well, this additional money would come from the profits that the endowment funds earned in the deals, but if all went badly, they would be liable for raising the money.

Harvard, with about $4 billion in private-equity deals in 2008, is a case in point. Because it had an unfunded commitment of approximately $1 billion for capital calls, it attempted to reduce its exposure by selling some of its private-equity participations to so-called secondary funds. But it had to offer to sell them at as much as a 35 percent discount, and, even at that price, it found no buyers in 2008.

Hedge funds, another main channel for alternative investment, provide somewhat better liquidity, but they also can restrict withdrawals by "gating" their fund. Harvard, for example, invested half a billion dollars in a hedge fund called Sowood Capital. But in July 2007 the hedge fund got caught in a complex series of arbitrage trades involving credit-default swaps that wiped out more than half of its capital and, when it couldn't meet lenders' demands for more collateral, it turned over its remaining asserts, including what was left of Harvard's money, to another hedge fund, Citadel Investment Group, which then suspended redemptions.

The other alternative-investment channel in the Swensen strategy is physical assets, including huge tracts of land and real estate. Turning such assets into money can, however, be difficult. Consider what happened to Calpers, the giant pension fund of the California Public Employees' Retirement System, when it sunk part of its portfolio investment in undeveloped residential and timber land in Arizona, Florida, and California. As home prices fell in 2007-08, Calpers was unable to sell properties for anywhere near the price it paid and, as it borrowed to finance these purchases, it wound up with a 103 percent loss.

Illiquidity is not a problem when notional prices go up in the boom years. When the bubble burst in 2008, however, those prices proved to be largely a mirage. Endowment funds' lost more than $50 billion.

As it turns out, the three main pillars of the diversification—private-equity participations, hedge funds, and physical assets—depend on the same variable: credit. When credit became less available in the financial meltdown, these alternative investments rapidly shed their notional value.

What of Swensen himself? Yale announced a 13.4 percent loss to its $22.5 endowment fund in October 2008 in its "marketable securities." But that $3 billion loss did not include its illiquid investments, including those outsourced to private-equity funds, which constituted more than two-thirds of its portfolio. Yale President Levin said it is difficult to know exactly how much the university has lost in investments that "are not traded on a daily basis and are difficult to value with precision."

Swensen shrugged off that problem in February 2009, noting http://www.propublica.org/article/yales-financial-wizard-david-swensen-says-most-endowments-shouldnt-try-to-b: "We only mark the portfolio to market once a year, on June 30," and adding that even this annual reckoning is done merely for financial disclosure and future planning purposes. If so, such willful blindness means that despite massive write downs at private-equity houses in

2008, Yale will not know how it has done on two-thirds of its portfolio until June 30, 2009. Swensen's once-a-year tactic, even if it is intended to show his calm in the eye of a financial storm, reflects the academic disconnect between the notional and realizable value of illiquid assets.

The real issue underlying the Swensen strategy is what the purpose of an endowment fund is. If it is to gamble on creating a jackpot large enough for a university to finance large-scale future expansion, his strategy may make sense, as it promises long-term profits. But if its purpose is to assure an institution's continuity in bad as well as good times, the strategy may be inappropriate, especially if in times of crises, when other money raising is diminished, a university may have to borrow enormous sums to meet capital calls from private-equity houses. Unfortunately, such considerations of purpose tend to be drowned out by the alluring, sweet-sounding tune of a pied piper.

[5]
Wizards of Japan

Since 2008 the US Federal Reserve Bank has made money the new fashioned way. It prints it electronically by sending electronic transmissions to major banks crediting their account with dollars in return for the purchase from them of US government bonds. This wizardry is called quantitative easing, or QE. QE has now created some $3 trillion (or about one-quarter of the GNP.) By buying up bonds with this magic money, the Fed lowered short-term interest rates to nearly zero. This meant that big banks could get money for almost nothing whereas some 30 million people with savings earned virtually no money on their nest eggs. This exchange did so little to stir the American economy that in mid September 2011, four years after the 2008 crash, the Fed put a new twist on QE: selling short term bonds and buying long term ones to lower longer term rates until they also approach zero. Despite this massive manipulations, unemployment remains over 9%, and there is almost no growth in the private sector.

If this sad tale sound familiar, it is because two decades ago the wizards of Japan invented the magic money solution of QE. Japan's bubble of 1989 indeed adumbrated the American bubble of 2008.

Fueled by low-interest mortgages, real estate prices in Japan had risen so high that by the end of the 1980s just the land under the Imperial Palace in Tokyo was nominally worth more than all the real estate in California. Then, in late 1989, the bubble burst and real estate prices plummeted, leaving Japan's financial institutions saddled with toxic mortgages and facing bankruptcy.
Despite the common misconception that the Japanese government neglected the crisis, it intervened from the outset. In 1990, the Japanese Central Bank cut interest rates until they reached absolute zero. So borrowing money was free for banks. Nevertheless the Japanese stock market continued its fall, with the Nikkei index going from a high of 40,000 in 1989 to a low of 12,000 in 2001. So did real estate, which lost 80 percent of its value during this period.

The government next tried all the classic Keynesian tactics, including spending and tax cuts. Between 1991 and 1998, it pumped 100 trillion yen into the economy through public works programs and, to further stimulate spending, it cut taxes by 2 trillion yen. All these measures succeeded in accomplishing was raising Japan's public debt to 100 percent of its GDP.

To deal with the ever more ominous threat of bank insolvency, the Japanese government injected public funds directly into Japanese banks, investing first in 1996 $100 billion and then in 1998, under the Obuchi Plan, another $500 billion to pay for bank loan losses, bank recapitalizations and depositor protection. The bail-out, which amounted to over 12 percent of GDP, resuscitated the individual banks but not the financial system . The banks, although on government life support, resisted lending out their new found capital. Paralyzed by the fear of losing their new found capital, many such banks became, in Japanese terminology, "zombies," since they were neither dead nor alive (at least in fulfilling their function of extending credit.) As a result, the money Japan pumped into its banks did not thaw the frozen system. By February 2001, the Bank of Japan had brought down the interest rate to zero. Then, in March 2002, it tried printing money under the now-familiar concept of quantitative easing. It simply used its newly created money to buy up Japanese government bonds. This "Rinban" made sure that interest stayed at zero and the banks were flooded with money. But the economy continued to sink, no matter how much it created.

It was not until 2002 that the Japanese economy, buoyed by the boom in China and other of its export markets, showed any growth. The moral of this financial Kabuki play is that government wizardry may produce an unintended lost decade.

[6]
The New Axis of Evil in Hollywood

In the Warner Bros. political thriller, *Syriana*, the villain is not al Qaeda, an enemy state, the mafia, or even a psychotic serial killer. Rather, it's the big oil companies who manipulate terrorism, wars, and social unrest to drive up oil prices. One doesn't need to look far to discover that the root-of-evil corporate villain is hardly atypical of post-Cold War Hollywood.

Consider, for example, Paramount's 2004 remake of the 1962 classic, *The Manchurian Candidate*. In the original film, directed by John Frankenheimer, the villain-behind-the-villain is the Soviet Union, whose nefarious agents, with the help of the Chinese Communists, abduct an American soldier in Korea and turn him into a sleeper assassin. In the new version, the venue is transposed from Korea in 1950 to Kuwait in 1991, and the defunct Soviet Union is replaced as the resident evil. The new villain is—you guessed it— the Manchurian Global Corporation, an American company loosely modeled on the Halliburton Corporation. As the director, Jonathan Demme, explains in his DVD commentary, he avoided making the Iraqi forces of Saddam Hussein (who the US was battling in the time frame of the movie) the replacement villain, because he did not want to "negatively stereotype" Muslims. Not only were neither Saddam Hussein nor Iraq mentioned in a film about the Iraq-Kuwait war, but the Manchurian corporation's technicians rewire the brains of the abducted US soldiers with false memories of al-Qaeda-type jihadists so that they will lay the blame for terrorist acts committed by American businessmen on an innocent Muslim jihadist.

Why don't the movies have plausible, real world villains anymore? One reason is that a plethora of stereotype-sensitive advocacy groups, representing everyone from hyphenated ethnic minorities and physically handicapped people to Army and CIA veterans, now maintain a liaison in Hollywood to protect their image. The studios themselves often have an "outreach program" in which executives are assigned to review scripts and characters with representatives from these groups, evaluate their complaints, and attempt to avoid potential brouhahas.

Finding evil villains is not as easy as it was in the days when a director could choose among Nazis, Communists, KGB, and Mafiosos. Still, in a pinch, these old enemies will serve. For example, the 2002 apocalyptic thriller *Sum of All Fears*, based on the Tom Clancy novel, originally had Muslim extremists exploding a nuclear bomb in Baltimore.

Paramount decided, however, to change the villains to Nazi businessmen residing in South Africa to avoid offending Arab-American and Islamic groups. Yet, even if aging Nazis lack any credible "outreach program" in Hollywood, no longer can they be creditably fit into many contemporary movies. "The list of non-offensive villains narrows quickly once you get past the tired clichés of Nazis," a top talent agency executive pointed out in an e-mail. "You'd be surprised at how short the list is."

For sci-fi and horror movies, there are always invaders from alien universes and zombies from another dimension, but even here it doesn't hurt if they are in the greed business. In the 2009 movie *Avatar*, a mining corporation is behind the use of avatars to destroy the environment, culture, and natives on the planet Pandora. For politico-thrillers the safest remaining characters are lily-white, impeccably dressed American corporate executives. They are especially useful as evildoers in foreign-based thrillers since their demonization does not run the risk of gratuitously offending officials in countries either hosting the filming or supplying tax or production subsidies. *Mission Impossible 2* thus replaced the Russian and Chinese heavies that populated the TV series with a Wall Street-type financier who controlled a pharmaceutical company that aimed to make a fortune by unleashing a horrific virus on the world. How? It owned the antidote. Here, as in other movies in this genre, businessmen's killings are not just figurative. Unlike other stereotype-challenged groups, CEOs and financiers, lacking a connection with the studios' outreach programs, have become an essential part of Hollywood's casting. They are the new all-purpose money demons.

***

Chapter VII
How Crazy Is Wall Street

The New York Times published an opinion piece on May 12, 2012, concerning the question of whether the rich, from a moral standpoint, are good or bad., "A recent study found that 10 percent of people who work on Wall Street are 'clinical psychopaths' and that they exhibit an 'unparalleled capacity for lying, fabrication, and manipulation.' " The vivid term "clinical psychopath" brings to mind the berserk buzz-saw-wielding investment banker played by Christian Bale in the film American Psycho. Since some 3.9 million people work in the financial-services industry, a clinically diagnosed horde of lunatics numbering almost 400,000 people would certainly be a matter of public concern, though it might only confirm some journalists' view of American capitalism.

It is fair to ask the provenance of this incredible "study." The New York Times cited its source as a March 12, 2011, , which attributes the psychopath data to an estimate made by Sherree DeCovny in CFA Magazine, in an article entitled "." She wrote that "studies conducted by Canadian forensic psychologist Robert Hare indicate that about 1 percent of the general population can be categorized as psychopathic, but the prevalence rate in the financial services industry is 10 percent."

The problem here is that Hare never conducted a clinical study of the financial-service industry, and never presented evidence that 10 percent of its members were psychopaths. John Grohol, the editor of World of Psychology, after the publication of DeCovny's article, asked Hare about the putative study. Hare told him, "I don't know who threw out the 10 percent, but it certainly did not come from me or my colleagues." The closest he came to such a claim was in a research paper he coauthored that analyzed the responses submitted by 203 corporate professionals from seven companies, none of which were on Wall Street. Nor were these 203 people randomly selected. He found that the answers of only eight people—approximately 4 percent of the sample—indicated psychopathic tendencies on a scale he had devised. Even though this was not a clinical study, the responses of these eight people, who might have not even worked in financial services, were transformed via the blogosphere into a supposedly scientific finding noted in one of our most respected newspapers that one tenth of those working on Wall Street are clinical psychopaths

The Times posted a correction a week later, noting that "an earlier version of this article misstated the findings of a 2010 study." As Ryan Holiday, author of Trust Me, I'm Lying: Confessions of a Media Manipulator, explained to me, "Headline-grabbing trend manufacturing such as this now dominates the pseudo-news cycle on the Web." The Internet is not known for its source-checking but Unfortunately, it is then only a short leap to the so-called newspaper of record, which was happy to serve up to the public this non-existing study, which like much else demonizes financiers, as a scientific finding. As a result, we now have mad men of Wall Street running amok in the public imagination.

Chapter VIII

Is The Government Out Of Control?

A bedrock principle of Anglo-Saxon jurisprudence is that there is a presumption of innocence, This should mean that if the government fails to find incriminating evidence in an exhaustive investigation, they cannot punish a person for a crime or confiscate his property. Yet, prosecutors have found ways to bypass the absence of evidence when it comes to Wall Street, Consider the case of Steven A. Cohen, the founder and owner of SAC Capital Advisors, a ten-billion group of hedge funds, No one can doubt that the six year investigation of him for inside trading qualifies as exhaustive.

It originated with a highly-plausible theory that his consistently high trading profits resulted from an orchestrated scheme of inside trading. To substantiate it, the SEC and Department of Justice sought the requisite evidence. They subpoenaed or otherwise managed to obtain 375 million pages of the trading records, correspondence and other documents of Cohen and his SAC funds. This massive trove of documents, however, did not yield any usable evidence that Cohen was involved in inside trading. The Feds also employed surreptitious means, including planting court-approved listening devices in Cohen's home to intercept his conversations with his top lieutenants used plan his funds' weekly trading strategy, and planting a mole in his organization. The mole was Richard C.B Lee, a former SAC employee, who, wearing a wire, proposed to Cohen various "trading ideas" based on inside information (presumably scripted by his Fed handlers.). Despite the provocations, none of the bugging produced usable evidence against Cohen. Finally, as is not uncommon in Wall Street cases, prosecutors attempted to induce former and present SAC employees to testify against Cohen, including eight who had been themselves charged with using inside information, Even though five of them agreed to cooperate with the government, none were able to provide evidence that Cohen had known of their alleged inside trading, even when by proffering it might have spared themselves prison. As a result, the government had no evidence to support its theory in court. Despite this embarrassing absence of evidence against Cohen, the prosecutors did not give up. Instead, they shifted to plan B: targeting Cohen's corporation, SAC Capital in a two pronged attack.

The first prong was a Grand Jury indictment of Cohen's corporate alter ego, SAC Capital, for security and wire fraud. It alleged that SAC had encouraged its employees to seek illegally-obtained data by providing them with profit-sharing and then not properly enforcing its own rules against using inside information. SAC Capital, which denies this allegation, will have its day in court to defend itself.

The second prong was a civil forfeiture complaint charging that SAC Capital engaged in a money-laundering conspiracy. Such civil forfeiture complaints began as means of destroying the cash resources of drug traffickers. They allow the government to seize all the assets of a suspect without even proving that a crime has been committed. Since it is technically leveled against the asset itself, the government need only to assert is that the "preponderance of the evidence" shows that it is subject to forfeiture. When this complaint is tied to money-laundering it can be disastrous for a financial institution because the government can freeze or seize all its assets, including those funds loaned to it.. In the case of SAC Capital, the putative money-laundering stems from the allegation the illegal earning were investing in, and thereby intermingled with, SAC Funds. But even if this occurred, was it the sort of money-laundering in which profits from an illegal enterprise are disguised as profits from a legal one? None of the traders had to disguise their commissions, bonuses and performance compensation, nor did they represent them as anything other than trading profits. But the government does not actually need to prove there was money laundering since this a civil forfeiture complaint.

The lethal part of the civil forfeiture complaint was its scope, seeking not a specific amount but "any and all" assets of SAC Capital. At last count, according to its regulatory filings, SAC funds held some $51 billion in securities and loans from counter parties. To be sure, U.S. Attorney Preet Bharara currently is not seeking to freeze these assets, a freeze which could rip a Lehman-size hole in the counter parties, and he has agreed to a Court Protective order tying up about $5 billion of SAC's capital. But the government could change its mind at any time, since a footnote in the agreement states that the protective order does not limit the ability of United States to proceed with the seizure of all of SAC's assets at some future point. So a sword of Damocles l hangs over SAC Capital.

Even if it demolishes his corporate alter ego. Cohen may well survive the Federal wrecking ball. He is after all a billionaire many times over with an extensive art collection. My concern here is not the fate of Cohen or SAC Capital. It is with the government's expansive use of money-laundering charges in civil forfeiture cases when it is unable to find incriminating evidence.

About The Author

Edward Jay Epstein studied government at Cornell and Harvard, receiving his Ph.D. from Harvard in 1973. His master's thesis at Cornell was published as Inquest: The Warren Commission and the Establishment of Truth and became a national best seller; his doctoral dissertation at Harvard was published as News From Nowhere: The Selection of Reality on Television, and is today a standard textbook in media studies courses . He taught political science at MIT and UCLA before becoming a full time author. He lives in New York City. His website is www.edwardjayepstein.com